To Fred - Christ

Hope this book will be
like a "meeting of the minds"
(great ones!) Love,

Tom & Judy

Some
Remembered
Words

Some Remembered Words

Oscar Shoenfeld

Academy Chicago Publishers

Cover art: *Books With Yellow Onion and Pink Quartz*
        by Julia Anderson-Miller

Published in 1996 by
Academy Chicago Publishers
363 West Erie Street
Chicago, IL 60610

© 1996 Oscar Shoenfeld

Library of Congress Cataloging-in-Publication Data

Shoenfeld, Oscar.
    Some remembered words / Oscar Shoenfeld
    p.   cm.
    ISBN 0-89733-439-6
    1. Commonplace-books.   I. Title.
PN6245.S48   1996
082—dc20   96-25527
                                  CIP

I am much indebted to my old friends
Carlos Hudson and **George Scheer**
for their help with this manuscript.
George's unexpected death prevented
him from writing an introduction
to this book.

The real marriage of true minds is for any two people to possess a sense of humour or irony pitched in exactly the same key, so that their joint glances at any subject cross like interarching searchlights.

—Edith Wharton,
A Backward Glance

So perfect! A complicated thought perfectly expressed in an architecturally constructed sentence with the tension and interest steadily leading up to the stunning final three words.

The sentence gains interest when we note the sentence immediately following;

> I have had good friends between whom and myself that bond was lacking, but they were never really intimate friends; and in that sense Henry James was perhaps the most intimate friend I ever had, though in many ways we were so different.

Given James's epicene nature and Wharton's sexual appetite, the main thing they shared—even more than common literary judgements—is best expressed in an earlier sentence in the same memoir:

> In every society there is the room, and the need, for a cultivated leisure class . . .

This brilliant woman has expressed a sophisticated rationale for snobbery and that indeed is what she and Henry James shared.

The happiest destiny is never to have been born; and the next best, by far, is to return, as swiftly as may be, to the bourn whence we came.

>—Sophocles
>Quoted in John Clive,
>*Macaulay: The Shaping
>of the Historian*

Macaulay marked this passage in his own copy of Sophocles on the occasion of Macaulay's 35th birthday. The contemporary meaning of *bourn* comes mainly from Hamlet's line "the undiscover'd country, from whose bourn no traveller returns." But Sophocles' meaning—at least in the translated version—is even deeper; it is a beginning as well as an ending.

L ast of all Lord Beaconsfield—
Disraeli—came also . . . The
whole hall rises for him; the ap-
plause is deafening; the greeting
such as he is rightly proud of. It
was a common remark that Lord
Beaconsfield was looking uncom-
monly well. So he was; as long as
he thought people were looking at
him. The condition of this great
man's health is an affair of State,
and is discussed very much as Louis
XIV's bodily welfare was discussed
when he changed his shirts in public. Lord Beaconfield does not
change his shirts in public. He
finds it less embarrassing to effect

from time to time an exchange of what are sometimes called his principles . . .

—G.W. Smalley,
London Letters

Smalley was the London correspondent of the *New York Tribune* in the 1870s and 1880s and seemed to know everyone of importance in London. Many of his newspaper reports are included in the imposing two-volume edition of his works published in 1891 by Harper & Brothers. When I bought the two volumes for $2 in a secondhand bookshop in Northhampton, Massachusetts, nobody there, myself included, had ever heard of Smalley. Since then I have seen references to him: e.g., in the Henry James–Edith Wharton correspondence. The witty but mean-spirited dispatch quoted is a report on a speech by Disraeli at the imposing annual Guildhall banquet attended by 700 guests.

He discoursed on London . . . com-
plaining of the very houses amid
which he took his devious way.
They were built, he said, to tumble
down in ninety years. The tenant
had only a ninety-nine year's lease
from the landlord who owned the
ground; he could not afford to
build solidly and honestly; the ar-
chitect had learned how to run up
a wall which would stand just long
enough not to become the property
of the landlord; computing that the
wall should fall down before the
lease fell in . . .

  —Smalley, in an affection-
   ate tribute to his friend
   Thomas Carlyle immedi-
   ately after Carlyle's death
   in 1881

Today a house designed for almost a century's use
would seem to be extraordinarily well-built! Other
times, other standards!

... he went from book to book (for like all great readers he kept a dozen or two books going at the same time, using them according to his changing thought, or even to their random proximity to his momentary armchair or couch) ...
—Paul Horgan,
A Certain Climate

In this essay, Horgan is describing the reading habits of Bernard Berenson. It is a favorite quotation because it is also a description of my life-long reading habits. However, I am not in the same league with Berenson, since I rarely have more than three or four books going at the same time.

C ome and take choice of all my library and so beguile thy sorrow.

—Shakespeare,
Titus Andronicus,
Act IV, Scene I

This is the most beautiful of all the words I quote. I have always wished I could share this noble thought, but possessiveness about my books far exceeds my generosity.

So he passed over, and all the trumpets sounded for him on the other side.
—John Bunyan,
Pilgrim's Progress

And John Bunyan's words from *Pilgrim's Progress* are the most majestic of all the words I quote. I saw them on a gravestone in the cemetery of St. Nicholas Church, Sandhurst, Kent, England, where Peggy and I were staying with friends.

H ere sleeps in peace a Hampshire grenadier
Who caught his death by drinking
cold small beer

Soldiers be wise from his untimely
fall
And when you're hot drink strong
or not at all

An honest soldier never is forgot
Whether he die by musket or by
pot

In 1967, I found this epitaph on a worn stone on
the steps of Salisbury Cathedral, England. Many
years later, an old friend was showing me pictures

that he had taken on a trip to England, and he had photographed this gravestone. But the stone looked new and the lettering was clear and distinct. The stone must have been sufficiently popular for the authorities to take measures to make it available to tourists. Quaintness, I guess, is an important commodity in the tourist business.

I t is rather an attempt to convey something of the sheer beauty of Chess, its perfect harmony, its inexhaustible wealth of ideas . . . There are those who will go so far as to link Chess with Johann Sebastian Bach's fugues, because of its crystal clarity. I even had a German philosopher speak of Chess in terms of the Kantian *Ding an sich*. But let that pass. Nor should we worry too much about those so smitten with the inherent harmony of Chess as to compare it with the equally perfect harmony of the *sectio aurea* which the ancient Greeks and Romans endowed with an almost mythical quality.

However that may be, even among the less dithyrambic admirers of Chess there are many who will claim that the game is not only science but an art too. A science because you can fill many shelves with erudite theoretical works; an art because it gives its practitioners an opportunity of expressing their individual style and character.

All this may well be so, but I think we could never forget that whatever else Chess may be (or may be imagined to be), it certainly is a game that can have as satisfying and, alas, as time-absorbing an effect on its addicts as, say, music. Those who are once captivated will soon admit the truth of the old adage: 'No fool can play Chess, and only fools do.' But some of us will never tire of such folly, and to some of us it may indeed have become an obsession soon after we have mastered the rules of the game.

—Heinrich Fraenkel,
Adventure in Chess

Any serious chess player will agree whole-heartedly with Heinrich Fraenkel's description of what the game may be. Fraenkel wrote a marvel-ous chess column for many years for the English *New Statesman and Nation* under the name Aissac—which spelled backward is the presumed name of the Goddess of Chess, Cassia. Fraenkel might have added the statement attributed to Lessing: "Chess is too much work for pleasure and too much pleasure for work."

. . . the long variety of piano duets
with everyone's wife . . .
—Michael Holroyd,
Bernard Shaw, Vol. I:
The Search for Love

Since I am a male piano duet player, I savored
this description of the horny GBS, a very well-
trained musician, enjoying the beauty of the four-
hand repertoire, at the same time that he contin-
ued his almost endless pursuit of many women
friends, married or not; a pursuit from which the
end of sexual intercourse was always absent, usually to the chagrin of the women.

I have always loved to play piano duets, but I must confess that there is a special pleasure in playing beautiful music with an attractive female pianist, especially when we are snuggled close together on a piano bench really made for one.

Max Shachtman, the well known American follower of Leon Trotsky, had a famous debate with Earl Browder after the veteran General Secretary of the American Communist Party had been ousted by Stalin. Shachtman ended his rebuttal with:

'There,'—and pointing his finger at Browder seated on the other side of the stage—'but for an accident of geography, sits a corpse.'

This dramatic statement is an allusion—well-known to all attending the debate—to the fact that many of Browder's fellow Communist leaders, all long-time faithful followers of Stalin, had been executed by the Great Leader.

Both Browder's and Schachtman's comments are very good examples of wit in debating. Perhaps their debating ripostes cannot be called "brilliant" because they create only a kind of shocked amusement and not much real enlightenment.

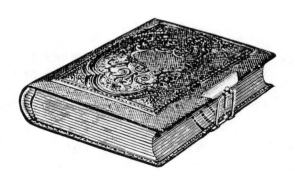

July 5, 1775

Mr Strahan,
    You are a member of Parlia-
ment, and one of that majority
which has doomed my country to
destruction. You have begun to
burn our towns and murder our
people. Look upon your hands!
They are stained with the blood of
your relations. You and I were long
friends. You are now my enemy,
and I am

                    Yours,
                    B. Franklin

William Strahan, like Franklin, was a printer, probably the most famous in England, and the subject of a biography called *Dr Johnson's Printer.* And like Franklin, Strahan was much involved in politics. When the war was over, the two resumed their friendship.

Political Tonalities. Major keys are optimistic. Minor keys are pessimistic. This dichotomy dates to the Renaissance, and it was restated with all the power of government by the first Commissar of Education of the Soviet Union, Anatoly Lunacharsky, who declared in his introductory speech at a Moscow concert on December 10, 1919:

> Major keys possess the characteristics of lifting a sound a semitone. By their exultant sense of joy such sounds elevate the mood; they cheer you

up. By contrast, minor keys droop; they lead to a compromise, to a surrender of social positions. Allow me, as an old Bolshevik, to formulate this observation: Major tonalities are Bolshevik music, whereas minor keys are deeply rooted in Menshevik mentality.

—Nicolas Slonimsky

Slonimsky comments on the above in his idiosyncratic *Lectionary of Music:*

Still, Bolsheviks love the music of Tchaikovsky, even though 85 percent of his works are set in minor keys. The resolution of this anomaly has been proposed by the learned theorists of the Society of Proletarian Musicians: Workers and Peasants enjoy the music of Tchaikovsky because it eloquently celebrates the funeral of the enemy class, the bourgeoisie. Q.E.D.

No Minor Chords

This is the title of Andre Previn's memoir of his days in Hollywood. The famous producer, Irving Thalberg, heard some music composed for one of his movies, music that he didn't like. When told that what he had heard was a chord in a minor key, he issued an edict that henceforth there were to be no more minor chords in any Thalberg movies.

"The Death Agony of Capitalism"

This was the title of a long essay by Leon Trotsky, written in 1937 and eloquently describing the last days of that now almost forgotten system of private enterprise.

Webb, complacently stroking his goatee beard, explained how under capitalism there might be as many as thirty or more varieties of fountain pen, whereas in the USSR we should find but one. A much more satisfactory arrangement. As he made the point, his bulbous eyes positively glowed behind the pince-nez.

—Malcolm Muggeridge,
Chronicles of Wasted Time

Muggeridge was a nephew-by-marriage of Beatrice and Sidney Webb and Sidney was explaining to the young man why socialism was so much superior to capitalism.

Once when I was lunching with him at a Greek restaurant in Percy Street he asked me to change places with him, which I cheerfully did. He explained that the reason for the change was that, from where he had been sitting, he looked straight at Kingsley lunching at an adjoining table; and the sight of so corrupt a face, he said, would spoil his luncheon.

Muggeridge again, describing a lunch with George Orwell. The object of Orwell's extreme distaste was Kingsley Martin, editor of *The New States-*

man, a leading British liberal magazine, and apologist for every crime committed by the Soviet dictator.

"Habent sua fata libelli" (Books have their own destiny).

The earliest attribution I have found for this adage is Terrentianus Maurus, A.D. 200. I first met with the quotation in the excellent introduction to the Everyman edition of Benjamin Franklin's autobiography, published in London in 1904 and simply signed W.M. I must have read this more than fifty years ago and I was so deeply impressed with the old adage that I finally commissioned an artist to design a beautiful bookplate based on it. I still use the bookplate.

I cannot doubt that you will unanimously assert the freedom of election, and vindicate your exclusive right to choose your representatives. But other questions have been started, on which your determination should be equally clear and unanimous. Let it be impressed upon your minds, let it be instilled into your children, that the liberty of the press is the palladium of all the civil, political, and religious rights of an Englishman, and that the right of juries to return a general verdict, in all cases whatsoever, is an essential part of our constitution, not to be

> controlled or limited by the judges, nor in any shape questionable by the legislature. The power of Kings, Lords, and Commons, is not an arbitrary power. They are the trustees, not the owners, of the state. The fee-simple is in us. They cannot alienate, they cannot waste . . .
> —"Dedication to the English Nation," the introduction to the *Junius Letters*, 1769

The identity of Junius is still not certain. These polemics were written in 1769, and addressed variously to the newspapers and different political notables of the day. I have always admired Junius's clear and effective prose and have long thought his letters the finest model of political polemic.

They had lost a villain and his new patrons had found a fool.
—John Dryden

I saw this quoted somewhere—I never did find the poem from which it presumably came—and was much impressed. I wait for an opportunity to use it on some turncoat.

I knew a gentleman who was so good a manager of his time that he would not even lose that small portion of it which the calls of nature obliged him to pass in the necessary-house; but gradually went through all the Latin poets in those moments.

—Lord Chesterfield
Quoted in Otto L. Bettman,
Delights of Reading

I must confess that when I was a boy, I had the same noxious habit. (Incidentally, I suspect that if I read with care all of Chesterfields's very many elegant letters of advice to his son, I would find virtually every Latin proverb I ever heard of used most appropriately.)

Archilocus, Greek poet who lived probably around the mid-seventh century BC and wrote short poems . . . His poetry survives in the quotations of later writers and some papyrus fragments. Ancient tradition says that he fell in love with Neobule, daughter of Lycambes, but her father forbade the marriage, and Archilocus avenged himself with such biting satire that father and daughter hanged themselves.

—*Oxford Companion
to Classical Literature*

Things have changed. Nowadays it is the poet who commits suicide.

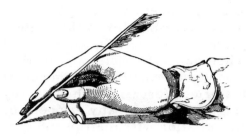

Surveying this watershed year of 1941, from which mankind has descended into its present predicament, the historian cannot but be astounded by the decisive role of individual will. Hitler and Stalin played chess with humanity. In all essentials, it was Stalin's personal insecurity, his obsessive fear of Germany, which led him to sign the fatal pact, and it was his greed and illusion—no one else's—which kept it operative, a screen of false security behind which Hitler prepared his murderous spring. It was Hitler, no one else, who determined on a war of annihilation against

Russia, cancelled, then postponed it, and reinstated it as the centerpiece of his strategy, as, how and when he chose. Neither man represented irresistible or even potent historical forces. Neither at any stage conducted any process of consultation with their peoples, or even spoke for self-appointed collegiate bodies. Both were solitary and unadvised in the manner in which they took these fateful steps, being guided by personal prejudices of the crudest kind and by their own arbitrary visions. Their lieutenants obeyed blindly or in apathetic terror, and the vast nations over which they ruled seemed to have had no choice but to stumble in their wake towards mutual destruction. We have here the very opposite of historical determinism—the apotheosis of the single autocrat. Thus it is, when the moral restraints of religion and tradition, hierarchy and precedent, are removed, the power to suspend or unleash catastrophic events does not devolve on the impersonal be- nevolence of the masses but falls into the hands of men who are iso- lated by the very totality of their evil natures.

—Paul Johnson,
Modern Times

An original and brilliant thesis—one that explains the key events of the twentieth century—all set out convincingly in this one eloquent, elegant para- graph.

Books seem to me to be pestilent things, and infect all that trade in them . . . with something very perverse and brutal. Printers, binders, sellers, and others that make a trade and gain out of them have universally so odd a turn and corruption of mind that they have a way of dealing peculiar to themselves, and not conformed to the good of society and that general fairness which cements mankind.
—John Locke, 1703

A harsh judgement indeed, but he leaves out the writer. "Anybody who doesn't write for money is a blockhead," said Dr Johnson, and why should we not assume that a writer can be as venal as the tradesman who prints, binds and sells his book?

One recent commentator has opined that Mathilde Ludendorff was mad. Conspiracy theories, however, cannot be dismissed on such grounds. Manifestly sane people have believed in them, including a former British Prime Minister, Benjamin Disraeli. They respond to a deeply felt human need to weave a pattern into events, eliminating chance, accident and contingency, and finding a human meaning, however sinister. They represent the story-telling impulse in usually pure form. Their development is dependent upon certain conditions being met. They flourish in the context of a Manichean mentality, which sees the world dominated by a conflict between sharply polarized forces of good and evil, hence their appearance during acute religious and political conflicts. That side of romanticism which was fascinated by everything out-of-the-ordinary, mysterious, occult and satanic gave them a new lease on life; Disraeli and Daumer belong here.

At the level of personal psychology, conspiracy theory can appeal to individuals who have difficulty coming to terms with certain aspects of their experience. A classic example is to be found in Hitler's *Mein Kampf*. He relates how from an early age his deepest conviction was nationalism, a love of the German people—the *Volk,* a term which suggests the common people, the mass. But when he met labouring people in Vienna, he was deeply troubled, for they did not live up to his image of them. They were feckless and disorderly, influenced by socialism and Marxism and therefore anti-national. Gradually, he tells us, he came to understand the reason: these basically good but simple Germans had fallen under the influence of the Jews, which spread like a poison through society. This insight restored his faith in his fellow-countrymen. General Ludendorff solved a similar personal problem in a similar way. In spite of his better knowledge, he came to explain the defeat of the glorious German army in 1918 in terms of a 'stab in the back' by the civilians back home— those civilians of course including socialists and Jews.

—William Stafford,
The Mozart Myths

I found this passage a brilliant description of the thinking behind many conspiracy theories, like concluding that Lee Harvey Oswald was an agent of the Soviet Union, the far Right, the CIA or the Mafia. Such theories always tell more about their authors than about the problem they purport to solve. Stafford disposes of many of the myths about Mozart and concludes by presenting two radically different theories about the nature of the incomparable genius, and then telling the reader that he cannot choose between the two theories. This reminded me of the statement attributed to Galileo that the three hardest words in any language are "I don't know."

Do You Sincerely Want To Be Rich?

This was the diabolically clever question that Bernard Cornfeld asked prospective salesmen seeking employment in his fabulously successful mutual fund sales organization, Investors Overseas Service. IOS later blew up in one of the great post-war financial scandals. The question was loaded; it meant that Cornfeld was telling the applicant that he—the applicant—really was smart enough to be rich and that the only reason he wasn't rich at this point was that he hadn't wanted to be badly enough. Thus, the applicant was suitably flattered and the conclusion was clear: now that he really did want to be rich, Cornfeld could tell him, then and there, how it could be done.

This question became the title of a book published by a *London Sunday Times* team, Charles Raw, Bruce Page and Godfrey Hodgson, after Cornfeld's empire had crumbled.

From distant fields the travellers who worked on commission came to London for conferences. These were old but lovable hands who had been at the business of selling books for a lifetime, and had taken on our 'line,' in addition to the half-dozen others they carried, in the hope that we might turn up a seller or two on which they would get ten per cent commission in their territories. They had been so long at their business that they behaved toward us like benevolent uncles, pouring out reams of advice written on the headed paper of third-class hotels

in provincial towns, or talking
volubly down the telephone—
charges reversed—while they explained why a certain jacket was
hopeless or a particular title too
late for the market or why one of
their customers must be allowed to
return for credit unsold stock of
one of our books. . . .
                    —Lovat Dickinson,
                    The House of Words

This quotation will probably be of no interest to
anybody except those who have been commission
salesmen for publishing houses, as I was for so
many years. Dickinson had been an English book
salesman himself before he started his own firm.
The sentences above, published in 1963, but describing the English bookselling world before
World War II, can certainly apply to that same
world I knew after the war. It is somewhat humili-
ating to read this rather patronizing denigration of
the work which we commission salesmen believed
was a thoughtful and important contribution to the
publishing world.

And further, by these, my son,
be admonished; of making
many books there is no end; and
much study is a weariness of the
flesh.

—Ecclesiastes

". . . of making many books there is no end . . ."
are the very well known words from the book of
Ecclesiastes, the teachings of the Prophet,
Qoheleth. To quote these words alone, however,
is to miss the meaning of the great book. The
Prophet merely observes that there is no end to
the making of books; but he then warns against
too much study. Earlier, he had said: "For in much

wisdom is much grief: and he that increaseth knowledge increaseth sorrow." But the editors of the twentieth-century New Revised Standard Version of the Bible comment that the book "fulfills a necessary role, warning against human hubris and preserving divine mystery."

The old people were not taken care of. This is another thing which people like to think now, that grandfathers and grandmothers had an honoured place in the cottage. In fact, when they got old they were just neglected, pushed away into corners. I even found them in cupboards! Even in fairly clean and respectable houses you often found an old man or woman shoved out of sight in a dark niche.

—Ronald Blythe,
Akenfield

Akenfield was a backwater, a rural village in Suffolk, England. Blythe wanted to know what life had been like in the village at the end of the nine-teenth century. He talked at length in 1967 with about fifty old villagers. The words above came from Marjorie Jope, aged seventy-nine at the time, who was a retired district nurse.

Blythe's book is the most effective answer I have ever seen to the sentimentalists who roman-ticize the place and the time, and the Marxists who insist that capitalism has resulted in the "impov-erishment" of the poor.

In all the history of music there has never been another man of such stupendous natural talents. It would be difficult, indeed, to match him in any of the other fine arts. He was the artist *par excellence*, moved by a powerful instinct to create beauty, and equipped by a prodigal nature with the precise and perfect tools . . . his ideas flowed like a cataract . . . his first thoughts, more often than not, were complete, perfect and incomparable . . . he stands above all . . . as a contriver of sheer beauty, as a maker of music in its purest sense.

—H.L. Mencken on Schubert
American Mercury, 1928

I was much pleased to find these words; Schubert has been my overwhelming favorite all my musical life and I have played, scores of times, all the marvelous four hand music and piano and violin sonatas with friends.

Mencken was a fine pianist, musician and amateur composer; his chamber music group, the Saturday Night Club, met regularly for forty years and Mencken, the impassioned leader, hardly ever missed a session. A good account of his musical life can be found in *H.L. Mencken On Music*, edited by Louis Cheslock. Cheslock had been the violinist of the group.

The following comes from a letter, reprinted in Cheslock's book, written in 1921 by Mencken to Fanny Butcher, the literary critic of the *Chicago Tribune*.

> **I'd rather have written any symphony of Brahms' than any play of Ibsen's. I'd rather have written the**

first movement of Beethoven's *Eroica* than the Song of Solomon; it is not only far more beautiful, it is also far more profound. A better man wrote it. . . . In music a man can let himself go. In words he always remains a bit stiff and unconvincing.

American commercial agriculture is doomed. With the melting away of farm land values there has disappeared the last sustaining hope of the American farmer, a hope which heretofore had permitted him to aspire to middle-class comfort and security. . . . Today farm income has collapsed . . . and there is not the slightest chance of restoring it. . . . He is, in short, for the first time in American history, a peasant bound to the soil because he can go nowhere else; and he is the helpless victim of high rents (not mortgage

charges because the property really is no longer his) and burdensome taxes . . .
—Louis M. Hacker,
The Farmer is Doomed

Louis M. Hacker was the Dean of Columbia University's School of General Studies and his special interest, as *The Reader's Encyclopedia of American Literature* states, "is the history and characteristics of American capitalism." Hacker's apocalyptic voice in the thirties was only one of the large chorus in American intellectual life.

Flora Thompson died in 1947 at the age of seventy, a writer who had produced a minor classic in the last years of her life, and about whom very little else is generally known.

Her work is in a genre of its own not altogether easy to describe, for it falls into no obvious category. Her three books, *Lark Rise, Over to Candleford,* and *Candleford Green,* which first appeared singly and are now published together as a trilogy under the title *Lark Rise to Candleford,* are not really novels, though fiction plays a part in them here and there. Nor are they autobiography pure and simple, for the personal element is evasive and oblique. They are better described, perhaps, as social history; though that, again, is a misleading name to give. They are more intimate, more personal, more alive than social history is usually allowed to be, for Flora Thompson dwells on the humble details which social historians either do not know, or else leave out. They are a simple yet infinitely detailed record of the life of the poor as it was lived in an obscure Oxfordshire hamlet in the eighteen eighties and nineties, all remembered from a child's experience, all faithfully set down, all true. It is precious as a record of something that has perished, though neither far away nor long ago, as well as for its literary quality, and for the fact that Flora Thompson herself was a cottage

child, born in poverty, who wrote
with a touch of genius of the life
she knew.

—Margaret Lane,
Purely for Pleasure

Who would not be eager to read Flora Thompson
after this introduction? I read this essay by Margaret Lane more than twenty-five years ago and
immediately ordered *Lark Rise to Candleford*. It
had never been published in the U.S. and I had to
wait until the book came from the Oxford University Press in England. Flora Thompson in her minor masterpiece allowed me to understand, for the
first time, something of the joys and pains of the
rural poor a hundred years ago and consequently
much widened my social vision.

And of course, I read all the other essays included in Margaret Lane's book, *Purely for Pleasure*. Lane is a most imaginative essayist. In an
essay on Jane Austen, she points out that Miss
Austen, while never writing a word of explicit de-

scription, somehow, magically, enables us to see clearly the physical character of the rooms and houses her people lived in. All of the essays in this book add an unexpected insight into the people she writes about and I regret that I haven't yet read anything else she has written.

No dearness of price ought to hinder a man from the buying of books, if he has the money demanded for them, unless it be to withstand the malice of the seller or to await a more favourable opportunity of buying. . . . We are not only rendering service to God in preparing volumes of new books, but also exercising an office of sacred piety when we treat books carefully. . . . And in the first place as to the opening and closing of books, let there be due moderation, that they be not unclasped in precipitate haste, nor when we have finished our inspection be put away without being duly closed.

For it behooves us to guard a book
much more carefully than a boot
. . . You may happen to see some
headstrong youth lazily lounging
over his studies, and when the
winter's frost is sharp, his nose
running from the nipping cold
drips down, nor does he think of
wiping it with his pocket-handker-
chief until he has bedewed the book
with the ugly moisture. . . . His
nails are stuffed with fetid filth as
black as jet, with which he marks
any passage that pleases him. He
distributes a multitude of straws,
which he inserts to stick out in different places, so that the halm may
remind him of what his memory
cannot retain. . . . Continually
chattering, he is never weary of
disputing with his companions,
and while he alleges a crowd of
senseless arguments, he wets the
book lying half open in his lap with
sputtering showers . . .

—Bishop De Bury,
Philobiblon, 1345

This is the classic work on book collecting. De Bury was a fanatical book collector and, just three months before he died at the age of 58, he finished the apologia for his mania. He first explained that the love of God was in wisdom and wisdom was in books; ergo, he had demonstrated his great piety by amassing his great library!

De Bury's heart however, is in the second half of the work, where he writes in loving detail about the fate of his collection and makes clear that dirty, careless readers would be forever barred from touching his precious volumes. The restrictions are spelled out, but sadly, all De Bury's forethought could not prevent his great library from being completely dispersed after his death. De Bury would hardly be consoled by the fact that his book has been printed in many different languages and editions in the six centuries since his death.

T he range of Aldus' activity during the first year of the new
century* is astonishing. He was
now printing in four languages . . .
his Greek texts included five ex-
ceptionally important first editions
of the fifth-century classical writers Thucydides, Herodotus, Xeno-
phon, Sophocles and Euripides. . . .
We must also reckon with the in-
flux of Latin classics—Virgil,
Horace, Martial, Cicero, Lucan,
Statius, Ovid and Catullus— . . .
Most important of all is the introduction, with the italic script, of

---

* *The sixteenth century—O.S.*

the octavo book-form, and its sub-
sequent use for publications in
Greek, Latin and Italian. A small
volume, mass-produced in editions
of up to three thousand copies, rea-
sonably priced and easily carried,
it seems a social extension of the
humanists' conviction that literature could enlighten wherever it
went, and the shameless haste with
which the model was copied is the
clearest proof of its success.
—Martin Lowry,
The World of
Aldus Manutius

Aldus (1450–1515) was the founder of the Aldine
Press, undoubtedly the greatest of all publishing
houses. He published large numbers of beautiful
books by the best authors, priced them low,* and
played a large part in disseminating the culture
admired by the great scholars of the Renaissance,
many of whom acted as Aldus's advisors.

---

* *Ironically, genuine Aldine Press books today fetch
high prices at auctions—O.S.*

Bologna, 28 October [1507] Aldus Manutius of Rome, many greetings:

I have often wished, most learned Manutius, that the light you have cast on Greek and Latin literature, not by your printing alone and your splendid types, but by your brilliance and your uncommon learning, could have been matched by the profit you in your turn drew from them. So far as *fame* is concerned, the name of Aldus Manutius will without doubt be on the lips of all devotees of sacred literature unto all posterity; and your memory will be—as your fame now is—not merely illustrious but loved and cherished as well, because you are engaged, as I hear, in reviving and disseminating the good authors—with extreme diligence but not a commensurate profit—undergoing truly Herculean labors, labors splendid indeed and destined to bring you immortal glory, but meanwhile

more profitable to others than to
yourself. I hear you are printing
Plato in Greek types; very many
scholars eagerly await the book . . .
—From a letter of
Erasmus to Aldus

Some scholars have called the whole period
"The Age of Erasmus," *so* central was he to what
has been called the "Transalpine Renaissance."
His tribute to Aldus appears in Huizinga's *Erasmus
of Rotterdam.*

The orator described the system of prostitution, which was paying its millions every year to the police of the city. He pictured a room in which women displayed their persons, and men walked up and down and inspected them, selecting one as they would select an animal at a fair. The man paid his three dollars, to a cashier at the window, and received a brass check; then he went upstairs and paid this check to the woman upon receipt of her favors. And suddenly the orator put his hand into his pocket and drew forth one bit of metal.

'Behold!' he cried. 'The price of a woman's shame!'

To the lad in the audience this BRASS CHECK was the symbol of the most monstrous wickedness in the world. Night after night he would attend these meetings . . . he pitched in to help the orator's campaign and . . . the Evening Post candidate was swept into office in a tornado of excitement, and did what all Evening Post candidates did and always do—that is, nothing. . . . So he learned the grim lesson that there is more than one kind of parasite feeding on human weakness, there is more than one kind of prostitution which may be symbolized by the BRASS CHECK.

—Upton Sinclair,
The Brass Check

Sinclair's books, particularly *The Jungle,* a graphic description of the horrors of Chicago's meat-packing plants in 1906, led to reform legislation. His books helped to persuade many a young person—

myself included—that capitalism was a reactionary and greedy system and that socialism was the only answer. Sinclair was in and out of the Socialist Party and in 1934, he was almost elected Governor of California on the Democratic ticket. He wrote more than eighty books which were very popular in Europe.

Only a naive romantic could have written his words. It apparently didn't enter Sinclair's head that both he, "the lad in the audience," and his eager readers, could possibly be stirred above all by the erotic images of the passage. But then, it was truly a romantic age: the Russian Revolution had not yet taken place. It would forever destroy all the utopian Socialist dreams of idealistic youth.

ETS 443-2 Studies in Cultural
Theories of Representation: Euro-
centrism, (Post)coloniality, Revolution.

Instructor: Mas'ud Zavarzadeh
TTh 11:30

The course inquires into the political economy of cultural representation and produces a marxist
critique of dominant knowledges.
Its analytical axes evolve around
the questions of class, historical
materialism, totality, race, and the

economics of the 'metropole' and 'periphery.' It also engages the problematics of the 'Asiatic mode of production'; the 'subaltern,' the geopolitics of 'Oriental despotism,' the politics of (Western) feminism and women of colour; the nation, and imperialism. One of the discourses of this inquiry is the relation between (de)colonization and (de)construction: what are effectivities and politics of bourgeois theory for emancipatory practices of transformative politics and for 'reading' (post)colonial texts (e.g., Derrida, 'Racism's Last Word,' Foucault, 'Iran: The Spirit of a World Without Spirit')? What, in other words, are the consequences of 'discursive politics' in the moment of the (post)colonial? Adjacent to this discourse, the course (re)opens the question of 'revolution' through a (re)turn to Fanon, Che Guevara,

> Malcolm X, Cabral, Teitleboim . . .
> 'Intifada,' A.N.C. . . .
>> —*The English Newsletter: Undergraduate News From the English Department, Syracuse University,* Vol. 1, No. 2, Nov. 1990; cited in the *New Criterion,* Feb. 1991, under the heading "From the archives of the academy."

Multiculturalism in full bloom!

It was one of those rare moments in history in which the atmosphere of life is lyrical and charged with hope, when man seems his own master, and his destiny secure.
—J.H. Plumb,
    "G.M. Trevelyan"

Every man can, I think, apply this sentence to his own favorite moment in history, and even more, to his own life.

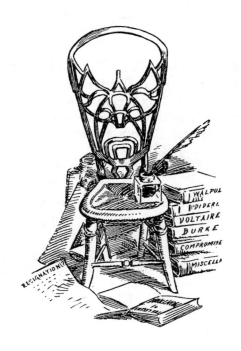

If I had Cervantes' genius, just as he purged Spain of the imitation of knights errant, I too would write a book purging Italy—indeed, the entire civilized world—of a certain vice, one which, with all due respect to the tameness of present customs, and perhaps in every other respect, is no less coarse and barbaric than any remnant of medieval savagery chastised by Cervantes. I mean the habit of reading or reciting one's own compositions to others. This very ancient custom was in past centuries a tolerable misery, since it was rare. But today, when everybody can write and when the hardest thing to find is someone who is *not* an author, this practice has become a scourge, a public calamity, one of life's newest hardships. I'm not joking when I say that because of this custom acquaintances have become suspect and friendships dangerous. For no matter where an innocent person goes, or when, he must fear being pounced upon and subjected on the spot (or dragged somewhere else) to the agony of hearing interminable prose or verses by the thousand. No longer under the pretext of soliciting the listener's opinion, which used to be the motive behind such readings, but rather solely and expressly to make the author happy by having someone listen to him, not to speak of the required praises at the end . . .

—Giacomo Leopardi,
Pensieri

Only a listener who has been subject to the same discomfort can appreciate this complaint. I think the discomfort is all the more acute on the part of those who suspect that they too, on more than one occasion, have subjected their friends to the same boredom by reading from their own writings. I have been both perpetrator and victim!

Finally, there is the chess. I refuse to apologize for its inclusion. Chess problems demand from the composer the same virtues that characterize all worthwhile art: originality, invention, conciseness, harmony, complexity, and splendid insincerity. The composing of those ivory-and-ebony riddles is a comparatively rare gift, and an extravagantly sterile occupation; but then all art is inutile, and divinely so, if compared to a number of more popular human endeavors. Problems are the poetry of chess, and its poetry, as all poetry, is subject to changing trends with various conflicts between old and new schools. Modern conventionalism repels me in chess problems as much as it does in 'social realism' or in 'abstract' sculpture ... The present collection of a few problems composed recently forms an adequate corollary to my later verse.

—Vladimir Nabokov,
Poems and Problems

Literate people can read and usually understand poetry. But even chess players—if they have not been devotees of the special world of chess problems—will have to work hard to solve Nabokov's problems!

Every man will dispute with great good humour upon a sub-ject in which he is not interested.
—Boswell quoting Dr Johnson

I know that I am not really interested in a subject when I find myself tolerant of someone else's dif-fering views and I suspect that such occasions are the only time when my opponents think of me as a pleasant fellow.

But, Sir, let me tell you, the no-blest prospect which a Scotchman ever sees, is the high road that leads to England!

Bayles Dictionary is a very useful work for those to consult who love the biographical part of literature, which is what I love most.

Also Dr Johnson's words, as quoted by Boswell. I found them both—amazingly enough—on the very same page of Boswell's biography, page 425 in Volume 1 of the original George Birbeck Hill edition.

I suspect that Johnson's apparent antipathy to Scotchmen—as he called them—was a pose. Elsewhere in the text and in his letters he alludes to them in a reasonable, favorable way. After all, Boswell himself—Johnson's friend, biographer and travel companion—was a Scot. Nevertheless, the comment, I think, is one of the great put-downs in English literature.

I was struck by the second quotation because I find biography that part of literature which I love the most. I think that if I enumerated the kinds of books I have read, biography would easily lead the list.

Pierre Bayle's *Dictionnaire historique et critique* was a famous work in its time, especially in France where it had great influence on the *philosophes*. As the *Britannica* points out, "three years before Locke wrote his *Letters On Toleration,* Bayle . . . argued that freedom of thought was a natural right, and that even an atheist was not necessarily a bad citizen."

W here is human nature so
weak as in the bookstore?
—Henry Ward Beecher

This comment—which was quoted in a bookmark
issued by the Harriet Beecher Stowe House in
Hartford, Connecticut—probably came from one
of the thousands of sermons and lectures that the
enormously popular nineteenth-century Con-
gregational clergyman delivered on every political and social question of the day. Not even a law-
suit charging adultery with one of his parishio-
ners—the jury disagreed on the verdict—could
affect his popularity. His sister Harriet wrote *Uncle*

Tom's Cabin, probably the most sensational and influential book ever published in this country.

How many times have I resolutely determined "just to look around" in a bookstore and then bought another book, sometimes a book I knew I wouldn't be reading for a long time to come? But then, literate people are divided between those who merely want to read and that smaller number who avariciously want actually to own the book they are reading or intend to read. Apparently, the famous preacher shared my greedy compulsion.

A word on the postal service . . . Prior to the First World War there were eight deliveries a day in London and six in provincial cities, running from 8:15 in the morning to 9:15 at night; there was one delivery on Sundays and public holidays, including Christmas. A letter posted during daylight hours would normally be delivered about three hours later; one sent at midnight would reach its destination by breakfast time the next morning . . .

> —Frederic Spotts,
> Preface, *Letters of Leonard Woolf*

How could letter writing not thrive with such help? And then, telephones were limited to a few rich households and businesses, typewriters were barely into use, there were no junk mail, no catalogues and no "communications industry." Today most college graduates have never written a personal letter in their lives and scores of paperback books are available to furnish a model for business letters, resumes, invitations, announcements, solicitations or any other written communication. Our century will not leave the same rich heritage of letters that we received from our forebears, and our descendants will be the poorer for the loss.

Blessed art Thou, Our God, King of the Universe, who hast not made me a woman.

This is one of the Morning Prayers recited by every Orthodox Jew. Originally, the words "heathen" and "slave" were also spoken. Nowadays, Conservative Jews have softened the Prayer to simply say ". . . who hast made me a Jew." It is a difficult heritage for many devout Jewish women, especially if they are also feminists.

. . . John Shakespeare held the office of High Bailiff, corresponding
to that of Mayor, in 1568–9 . . .
just at this time, a matter was in
dispute between the Corporation of
Stratford and a townsman . . .
and it was submitted for the arbi-
tration of . . . Henry Goodere of
Polesworth . . . then or later, little
William was packed off to Polesworth—a curious piece of good
luck for him and for us; for in all
England, outside London, there was
then, and was to be later, no place

> more feracious of poetic genius
> than Polesworth Hall . . .
> —Arthur Gray,
> *A Chapter in the Early
> Life of Shakespeare*

These words only hint at the imaginative thesis of Arthur Gray, M.A., Master of Jesus College, Cambridge, in his book, published in 1926 at the University Press in Cambridge. Gray tells us at the outset that he has no proof for his original idea; he claims only that it is a likely explanation for Shakespeare's sudden emergence in London in 1592 as the master of the English language and drama. He points out that Sir Henry Goodere, the master of the manor of Polesworth, brought into his service bright boys as pages. One such was the poet Michael Drayton:

> It does not appear that he attended any school, unless it were the school supported by Sir Henry. To Sir Henry he expressly acknowledges that he owed the most part

> of his education . . . he describes
> how his 'mild tutor' smilingly en-
> couraged him in his aspiration to
> be a poet . . .

Goodere knew Shakespeare's father and Gray guesses that young Will too became a page. There were more books in Polesworth Abbey, situated in Shakespeare's native Warwickshire, than in all of Stratford; with Drayton and the other pages, Shakespeare would have had a better education than was possible in Stratford. A key part of Gray's theory is his demonstration of the similarity between Shakespeare's nature settings and the forests and flowers surrounding Polesworth.

Gray gives us his admittedly speculative explanation of one of the great Shakesperian mysteries; where and how did the writer spend his adolescence and what kind of education did he have before he came to London? Arthur Gray has written a thoughtful and intriguing book. Now long out of print, it merits reprinting and discussion. S. Schoenbaum, the eminent Shakesperian scholar, referred to Gray's "crack-brained thesis" and wondered why a distinguished university press published it. Well, apparently the readers of Gray's manuscript at Cambridge University Press felt the same way I do about his work.

In the days when Lord George Gordon became a Jew, and was suspected of insanity; when out of respect for the prophecies, England denied her Jews every civic right except that of paying taxes; when the Gentleman's Magazine had ill words for the infidel alien; when Jewish marriages were invalid and bequests for Hebrew colleges void . . .

> —Israel Zangwill,
> *King of Schnorrers*

These were the opening words of Israel Zangwill's tales of Jewish life in London at the end of the eighteenth century. They tell of the tensions between the aristocratic Sephardic, mainly Spanish, Jews and the rich upstart German merchant Jews. It is a comic story of snobbery and servility, but, nevertheless, Zangwill's exotic Jews come to us as men of dignity, sensitivity and intelligence. I don't think that any formal English history explains, as does Zangwill, what life was like for London's Jews two hundred years ago.

I must confess that, as a Jew of Eastern European descent, I was rather gratified to learn that the German Jews—who looked down on Eastern European Jews when they came to America in large numbers in the nineteenth century, and indeed, even coined the word 'kikes' for them—were the object of similar scorn by the Sephardic Jews almost a century earlier.

The general problem was that the children tended to shout rather than sing, reflecting, in Frank's opinion, the lack of singing in the homes. More particularly, the Jewish children beginning to arrive in the city from Poland and Russia had a rasping nasal twang to their voices that proved almost impossible to eradicate. Culturally, these children and their parents were more attuned to stringed instruments than to singing, and as they replaced Germans and Italians on the city's lower East Side the Peoples Choral Union discovered that it could no longer re-

cruit a singing class there. On the
other hand the neighborhood's
Music School Settlement in which
David Mannes had begun to teach,
soon had tripled its violin class.
—George Martin,
The Damrosch Dynasty

Frank Damrosch was an eminent musician, the Superintendent of Music in the New York City public school system from 1897 to 1905 and the
founder in 1892 of the Peoples Choral Union and
also of the Institute of Musical Art, now the
Juilliard School of Music. David Mannes, his
brother-in-law, founded the Mannes College of
Music. The most famous members of the family
were Walter, the most popular conductor of his
time, and Frank and Walter's father Leopold, the
founder of the Oratorio Society and the New York
Symphony.

The impact of George Martin's statement of
fact is astonishing. Were the music critic of the
New York Times to say the same today, one can
imagine the charges of anti-Semitism and racism

that would be raised. When I was young, mention of racial characteristics—German love of order, Italian excitability, Scandinavian stoicism—was common. Frank Damrosch's opinion, formed almost a century ago, would now fall under the same ban as all generalization about national and racial characteristics.

I have never been able to see in what way music critics have contributed to cultural progress; although on the other hand, there is no denying that their writings have frequently delayed it.

—Harold Bauer,
His Book

Bauer was a world-famous pianist when I was young.

I have long felt the almost total irrelevance of music criticism and rarely read any. It is basically subjective without objective standards; hence the frequent phenomenon of two reviewers holding totally opposed views on the same piece of music or the same musical performance. Since some critics do indeed write brilliantly, it can and does happen that the quality of the writing becomes the decisive factor for the reader; the music itself is merely the excuse for the free rein of the writer's imagination.

Bauer adds to the thought the unfortunate fact that a negative review by a critic can adversely affect the fate of a piece of music or the career of a performer; music history is full of examples of even great music getting bad notices and disappearing from the repertoire after one or two performances, and only many years later reappearing when some fine musician happens on a score and insists on giving it a new hearing.

I have had many an argument with good friends who piously read the reviews and sometimes form their own opinions of the music based on what their favorite critics have to say!

Is it better to have the camel in side the tent pissing out or out-side pissing in?

　—Lyndon B. Johnson about
　J. Edgar Hoover. Quoted
　by Carol Gelderman,
　Louis Auchincloss

LBJ was the consummate master of political tactics as well as of the American vernacular. Unlike Franklin D. Roosevelt, his avowed master, LBJ failed with long-term political strategy. He had not prepared for a long and difficult war in Vietnam and was rejected by a public which could not accept a leader caught without a solution to a major problem. Tactics and strategy, no less in politics than in chess, are two connected but separate talents, and especially in the end game, a long-term plan is vital.

. . . he was what the French would call an étourdi, or Harley Street a borderline case: an eccentric; a scatterbrain; in the graphic folk-phrase, something of a crackpot . . . the Freudians could hardly hesitate to label him a maladjusted introvert with unbalanced thyroid and pituitaries. . . . All his life Boswell was teetering on the edge of complete sanity. . . . That mental instability which is the dominant Boswell note . . . many of Boswells own contemporaries . . . chant a contemptuous chorus of

'fool, blockhead, zany, lickspittle, buffoon' . . .
>   —D.B. Wyndham Lewis,
>   *The Hooded Hawk, or*
>   *The Case of Mr Boswell*

Servile and impertinent, shallow and pedantic, a bigot and a sot, bloated with family pride, a tale-bearer, an eavesdropper, a common butt in the taverns of London.
>   —Lewis quoting from
>   Macaulay's famous
>   intemperate attack on
>   Boswell

It should be said, in all fairness, that Lewis quotes these remarks about Boswell the better to refute them.

None of his judges, if I may say so respectfully, explains clearly how this deboshed* rake and lunatic managed to create in the years of

---

*Obsolete *or* archaic. *according to the OED, but mean-ing* debauched—O.S.

> his alleged collapse, at least two
> works, in virile comely English,
> which will give delight as long as
> the language endures, and reveal
> the literary artist on almost every
> page.

A succinct rebuttal to Boswell's almost forgotten critics!

D.B. Wyndham Lewis (1894–1969), as *The Oxford Companion to English Literature,* 5th Edition, points out, should not be confused with *Percy* Wyndham Lewis (1882–1957). Percy, an artist and writer, is remembered today as a leader of the 1912–1915 avant-garde Vorticist movement, a friend of Ezra Pound, and an admirer of Hitler and the Nazis. The *Oxford Companion* has an extensive article on Percy, but a mere reference to D.B. as "the Catholic biographer."

D.B. apparently had at his command hundreds, or thousands, of archaic words like "deboshed." One must look up each word and then discover that each fits in precisely with Lewis's meaning and no more modern word would have sufficed. Reading him, I did appreciate, more than ever before, the incredible richness of the English language and realize how much of it is no longer part of our daily vocabulary. I am certain that D.B. had a good deal more to tell us than his trendy namesake, and that the *Oxford Companion* has not dealt adequately with an original and talented writer.

The matter of Malraux's Great Thoughts is likewise one on which judgement can be passed too hastily. One problem is that Malraux is a lifelong allusionist. In private conversation his allusionism confers upon the listener a sense of privileged euphoria. It is as if we were plugged into a central telephone exchange and were eavesdropping without regard for place, period, or plausibility, on two hundred conversations at the same time. The builder of the Great Pyramid is on the line to Cezanne, Socrates has a long-distance hook-up with Robespierre, Nehru swaps

epigrams with Montezuma. Two
hours later we reel out of the house
with cerebral cramp and cannot
remember a word.

> —John Russell,
> "The Malraux Show"
> *New York Times*
> *Review of Books*, 1976
> Reprinted in *Reading*
> *Russell,* 1989

Russell shows us that Malraux exaggerated, in-
vented and lied; nevertheless who would not want
to witness such brilliant displays of transcenden-
tal imagination?

Another example of cavalier disregard for
the pedantic truth can be found in Harold Laski's
letters to Justice Holmes. I found each letter as
fascinating as Holmes did; questions about the lit-
eral truth of each statement are subsumed under
the spell of imagination and the reader regrets the
eventual ending of each long letter, a letter which
generally deals more than adequately with no
fewer than a dozen subjects.

The true 'glory' of the Revolution lies not in the minimum of violence which was necessary for its success, but in the way of escape from violence which the Revolution Settlement found for future generations of Englishmen . . . it is England's true glory that the cataclysm of James's overthrow was not accompanied by the shedding of English blood either on the field or on the scaffold. The political instincts of our people appeared in the avoidance of a second civil war, for which all the elements were present. . . .

The Convention Parliament of February, 1689 . . . by wise compromise . . . stanched for ever the blood feud of Roundhead and Cavalier, of Anglican and Puritan . . . Whig and Tory, having risen together in rebellion against James, seized the fleeting moment of their union to fix a new-old form of Government, known in history as the Revolution Settlement. Under it, England has lived at peace within herself ever since . . . . its fundamentals have remained to bear the weight of the vast democratic superstructure which the nineteenth and twentieth centuries have raised upon its sure foundation. Here, seen at long range, is 'glory,' burning steadily for 250 years: it is not the fierce, short, destructive blaze of *la gloire.*

The expulsion of James was a revolutionary act, but otherwise the spirit of this strange Revolution was the opposite of revolutionary. It came not to overthrow the law but to confirm it against a law-breaking King. It came not to coerce people into one pattern of opinion in politics or religion, but to give them freedom under and by the law. It was at once liberal and conservative; most revolutions are neither one nor the other, but overthrow the laws, and then tolerate no way of thinking save one. But in our Revolution the two great parties in Church and State united to save the laws of the land from destruction by James; having done so, and having thereby become jointly and severally masters of the situation in February, 1689, neither the Whig nor the Tory party would suffer its clients to be any longer subject to persecution, either by the Royal power, or by the opposite party in the State. Under these circumstances the keynote of the Revolution Settlement was personal freedom under the law, both

> in religion and in politics. The most
> conservative of all revolutions in
> history was also the most liberal . . .
> —G.M. Trevelyan,
>   *The English Revolution:*
>   *1688-1689*

History has called it "The Glorious Revolution" because William, the Dutch Prince, replaced James as king with no bloodshed. Trevelyan's simple explanation of the most profound political change in the modern world—the emergence of a democratic society—is also basic to an understanding of American society. The forefathers of the Founding Fathers were among the very makers of The Glorious Revolution and the democratic character of the new American Republic has its roots in the ideas and accomplishments of the earlier English political society.

I discovered Trevelyan's *History of England* during the early '30s while browsing through New York's secondhand book center with its scores of bookstalls on Fourth Avenue. I had never heard of Trevelyan when I saw this nice cloth-bound copy, priced at ten cents, and read a few pages. I was hooked and became a devotee of narrative history then and there. Trevelyan's work was indeed the very model of such historical narrative and I can't imagine any other kind of historian telling the story of so complicated a political event with such clarity and vigor.

Trevelyan was enormously popular during the '20s, but narrative history became distinctly out of fashion with the intellectuals and the Academy after the Depression. By the '90s, Trevelyan was an almost forgotten name and his best-selling *History* was long out of print. I couldn't find a copy of his book in any New York or London secondhand bookshop early in 1995. But then, I am consoled by the old Latin adage, *Habent Sua Fata Libelli*: Books have their own destiny.

. . . Our Navy Department purchased a number of merchant vessels, yachts, and tugs, and the work
of converting and arming them was
immediately begun. The most sig-
nificant of our preparations for
war was the chartering of the
American liners *St. Paul* and *St.
Louis*, and a few days later, of the
New York and *Paris*. These mag-
nificent vessels, owing to their
speed and displacement, proved
themselves invaluable as scouts
and transports. Though the price
agreed upon, $2,500 a day for
each, seemed excessive, the service
they rendered the nation more than

outweighed their cost. Four of our coastwise steamers, belonging to the Morgan line, were purchased, and renamed the *Yankee, Dixie, Prairie* and *Yosemite.* These vessels were partly manned by officers and men of the Naval Militia and rendered very efficient service. The Navy has also been increased by the purchase of several war vessels abroad. . . .

—W. Nephew King, Lieut. USN, *The Story of the Spanish American War and the Revolt in the Philippines*

This large and elaborate book was "Illustrated From Drawings In Black And White Photography Taken At The Front And Paintings By The Best Artists. For the Army, O.O. Howard Major-General (Retired) USA; For the Navy, Robley D. Evans, Captain, USN. Published by Peter Fenelon Collier & Son, New York 1900."

Thus we prepared for war in that guilt-free time, so long ago! I found this old book in a second-hand bookshop and as I read it, realized for the first time, the enormous pride the country took in becoming a great imperial power. With fewer than 300 battle casualties, it is small wonder that the Spanish American War was the most popular war that this country had ever fought.

S mith tells a strange story of the contracts offered to ship-owners a little over a hundred years ago. The French government, he said, wanted ships . . .

—Jennifer Glyn,
Prince of Publishers: A Biography of the Great Victorian Publisher George Smith

. . . to dispatch a large body of convicts—the product of the recently suppressed Commune—to New Caledonia, and our firm had a chance of getting the job. Bilbrough* had already filled some sheets of paper with calculations. He proposed with his usual energy that we should start for Paris that evening. We went, and passed several days in negotiations. Whether we should have secured the contract I cannot tell; but we abandoned the attempt directly we learnt what the plans of the French government were. The general arrangements for the unfortunate convicts were harsh in every detail to the point of inhumanity. But one feature of the arrangements was quite too much for me. The French officials required that, athwart the compartment prepared for the convicts, should be iron plates extending from the keel to the deck, perforated with loopholes for light cannon, or for rifle fire. On any disturbance arising amongst the convicts the guards

---

* Smith's partner—O.S.

were to instantly fire through these loopholes, and to maintain their fire until every convict was shot down. . . . The contract was large and profitable; some eighteen or nineteen ships would have been required. But neither Bilbrough nor I could tolerate the idea of our vessels being turned into slaughter-ships, and we withdrew from the negotiations. . . .

> —George Smith,
> *Recollections of a*
> *Long and Busy Life*

George Smith was the director and principal owner of the enormously successful nineteenth-century publishing house, Smith & Elder; by 1866, according to Glyn, the firm employed 200 clerks and turnover reached £627,129. Smith was involved in many other enterprises, including ship-owning.

Smith's revelation tells us of the vengeful reprisals the Nationalist Government took against the defeated Communards. Eighteen thousand Parisians died and seven thousand were deported to the desolate islands. The Paris Commune is still revered in radical history and Smith's story brought back my memory of the time, long ago, when I was deeply stirred by the tale of that doomed revolt.

. . . One of [George] Washington's
confidential correspondents, Congressman Joseph Jones, . . . warned
that 'dangerous combinations in
the army' were using 'sinister
practices' to tear down Washington's reputation so that 'the weight
of your opposition will prove no
obstacle to their ambitious de-
signs.' Jones believed that the plot
was likely to succeed.

. . . In that year of 1783, the
efforts of the United States to establish a republican government
were unique in the world. Modern
history presented no evidence that

people could rule themselves . . .
it was generally believed in Europe
that efforts at popular rule could
only eventuate in anarchy and
chaos. As Washington paced in
perplexity, anarchy and chaos
seemed about to overwhelm America. Was it not his patriotic duty,
as Hamilton said, to accept the inevitable, as he had often done on
physical battlefields? And what of
his ambitions? In a world of kings,
why should not George Washington also be a king? He was later to
thank the Ruler of the Universe—
'the Greatest and Best of Beings'—
for having led him 'to detest the
folly and madness of unbounded
ambition.'

. . . He summoned a meeting
of his own for the following Saturday, March 15, 1783. This was
probably the most important single
gathering ever held in the United
States. Supposing, as seemed only
too possible, Washington should

fail to prevent military interven-
tion in civil government?

. . . When he strode on the
stage . . . he saw . . . on the faces of
his gathered officers . . . resent-
ment and anger. . . . He urged the
officers not 'to open the flood gates
of civil discord, and deluge our ris-
ing empire in blood' . . .

Washington had come to the
end of his prepared speech but his
audience did not seem truly moved. He clearly had not achieved his
end. He remembered that he
brought with him a reassuring letter from a congressman. He would
read it. He pulled the paper from
his pocket, and then something
seemed to go wrong. The General
seemed confused; he stared at the
paper helplessly. The officers
leaned forward, their hearts con-
tracting with anxiety. Washington
pulled from his pocket something
only his intimates had seen him
wear; a pair of eyeglasses. 'Gentle-

men, . . . you will permit me to put on my spectacles, for I have not only grown gray but almost blind in the service of my country.'

This homely act and simple statement did what all Washington's arguments had failed to do. The hardened soldiers wept. Washington had saved the United States from tyranny and civil discord. As Jefferson was later to comment, 'The moderation and virtue of a single character probably prevented this Revolution from being closed, as most others had been, by a subversion of that liberty it was intended to establish.'

—James Thomas Flexner,
*Washington: The
Indispensable Man*

This detailed biography made me know Washington as truly the first and greatest of the Founding Fathers, the essential figure in the birth of the new republic. I owe a permanent debt to James Thomas Flexner; he enabled me to escape the jaded cynicism of my century, a time that had largely forgotten the flesh and blood figure of the leader of the War for Independence and the first President of the United States.

'And are you still as fond of music as ever, Mr Pontifex?' said Miss Skinner to Ernest during the course of lunch.

'Of some kinds of music, yes, Miss Skinner, but you know that I never did like modern music.'

'Isn't that rather dreadful?— Don't you think you rather'—she was going to have added. 'ought to?' but she left it unsaid, feeling doubtless that she had sufficiently conveyed her meaning.

'I would like modern music, if I could; I have been trying all my life to like it, but I succeed less and less the older I grow.'

> 'And pray, where do you con-
> sider modern music to begin?'
> 'With Sebastian Bach.'
> —Samuel Butler,
> *The Way of All Flesh*

Butler's semi-autobiographical novel was published posthumously in 1903. Butler was an ac-
complished musician and composer—as well as a
painter who exhibited at the Royal Academy, and
the author of attacks on Darwin's theory of Natural Selection. His principal fame came from his
novel *Erehwon,* the queerest anti-machinery Uto-
pia I ever read. But *The Way Of All Flesh* is a
masterpiece; I have just reread it, sixty odd years
after my first reading, and once again I found it
absorbing.

Butler is to be forgiven his absurd rejection
of Bach; God knows what my likes and dislikes
will look like one hundred years from now!

. . . I authorized criminal action
against the Dunne brothers and
others, under the Smith Act. I believed that under my direction the
case could be tried fairly and
would not result in a spate of pros-
ecutions for sedition as in the
twenties, immediately after the last
war. The Smith Act, adopted in
1940, was the first peacetime sedition law since the notorious stat-
ute of 1798, which expired in two
years and was not renewed, under
which critics of the administration
of John Adams, particularly newspaper editors, were sent to jail,
sometimes for merely jeering at the

President . . . This particular law [the Smith Act] made it criminal to advocate destruction of the government by force or violence . . . I thought that this provision might be declared unconstitutional under the First Amendment of the Constitution, which protected freedom of utterance. And, with some reluctance, I authorized a prosecution so that the law would be tested at the threshold, and taken to the Supreme Court, where it would, I hoped and believed, be knocked out.

. . . the trial was fair, there were a number of acquittals, and although the Dunnes and several others were convicted, the sentences were comparatively light, running from a year and a day to sixteen months. . . . The judgment was sustained on appeal to the Circuit Court of Appeals; but to my surprise the Supreme Court refused to review it . . .

I have since come to regret that
I authorized the prosecution. . . .
The two Dunne brothers and their
twenty-seven associates were the
leaders of the Trotskyist Socialist
Worker's Party, a little splinter
group, which claimed 3000 members, and by no conceivable stretch
of a liberal imagination could have
been said to constitute any 'clear
and present danger' to the government, which, it was alleged, they
were conspiring to overthrow . . .
                    —Francis Biddle,
                        In Brief Authority

Francis Biddle was Solicitor-General of the United
States. Some years after the publication of this
book the Supreme Court did declare the Smith Act
unconstitutional. In the meantime, the eighteen
defendants who had been convicted served their
sentences. I was the youngest of the prisoners and
served my time in the Federal Correctional Insti-
tution in Danbury, Connecticut.

No government official ever suggested a pardon for those who had served time for conviction under an act subsequently declared unconstitutional and hence null and void. After Biddle's book was published, I sent a letter to my old friend Sidney Hook, telling him of Biddle's remarks. Hook intervened on my behalf with one of of President Kennedy's advisors, who wrote to me, sometime in 1963, that he would recommend to the President, at the earliest opportunity, that the eighteen be pardoned. The President was assassinated in November 1963, and that was the end of the proposal for pardon.

<blockquote>

They laid Jesse James in his grave and Dante Gabriel Rossetti died immediately. . . .

—Thomas Beer,
The Mauve Decade

</blockquote>

Is it possible to read these opening words and not continue? I did just that fifty years ago—never finished the book. I found the work elaborately mannered and overwritten. But for all these years, I remembered the startling first sentence, the juxtaposition of the two totally separate incidents. I had read enough of the book to realize that Beer was noting all the disparate events that go to make up any historical period. Each one was like a painter's dot in a pointillist painting, making no sense by itself, but becoming part of Beer's carefully constructed picture of the 1890s.

I tried to read the book recently, but had, as well as I can remember, the same reaction as earlier. I am not sure whether this is a justified criticism of Beer or, rather, an admission of my own limitations.

W hen France was riven by the bitter factional struggles over the Dreyfus case, Adams closed ranks with the conservative members of his Paris circle who regarded the defense of Dreyfus as part of a Jewish conspiracy to discredit the army and the Catholic church. His anti-Semitism became so extravagant that his friend Hay* remarked that when Adams 'saw Vesuvius reddening the midnight

---

* *John Hay—Lincoln's secretary, later Ambassador to England and McKinley's Secretary of State—O.S.*

air he searched the horizon to find a Jew stoking the fire.'

> —Ernest Samuels,
> *Selected Letters of
> Henry Adams*

L ansing* had once been appointed to head a delegation that was sent to New York after the great San Francisco fire [of 1905] to appeal for funds to rebuild the city. A banquet was given by the New York banking fraternity at which such distinguished financiers as Otto Kahn and Jules Bache delivered speeches glorifying the profession which kept the world solvent. Finally, the Chairman asked Lansing to give his views on the attributes that made for a great banker. Lansing rose and made the shortest banquet speech ever uttered. It consisted of one word:

---

* *Lansing Mizner, San Francisco banker—O.S.*

'Circumcision.' The New York
bankers lent San Francisco all the
money it required and did it in a
gale of laughter.
    —Anita Loos,
      Kiss Hollywood Good-Bye

Lansing was the brother of Loos's very close friend Wilson Mizner.

I quote both Adams and Loos lest any reader not understand that anti-Semitism, even before race prejudice, was the common bond of almost all Christians well into the twentieth century. Many a rich or educated Jew, anxious to be assimilated into the Christian world, was guilty of the same prejudice. Kahn and Bache were German Jews, among whom anti-Semitism was not uncommon; indeed they were the very inventors of the pejorative word *kike* to describe the Eastern European Jews who came in a later wave of immigration.

Henry Adams was the snob supreme and it was inevitable, I suppose, that he should be a ferocious anti-Semite. I haven't read any evidence of anti-Semitism in Anita Loos's amusing and sometimes brilliant writings.

What we fondly call a 'knowledge explosion' is probably not even an explosion of data but, rather, of printout.

We can all agree [with Dr Johnson's dictum] that the knowledge that one is to be hanged in a fortnight concentrates the mind wonderfully. The economist Paul Rosenstein-Rodan named the effect of this knowledge 'the tremble factor.' It is a dreadful but essential benefit to the independent sector, and the state sector has rarely faced it. One of the most effective uses to which the tremble factor has ever been put was in the building practices of ancient Rome. For when the scaffolding was removed from a completed Roman arch, the Roman engineer stood beneath. If the arch came crashing down, he was the first to know. His concern for the quality of the arch was intensely personal, and it is not surprising that so many Roman arches have survived.

—John Silber,
Straight Shooting

Dr Silber, president of Boston University and a well-known political conservative, ran an independent campaign in 1990 for the Democratic nomination for governor of Massachusetts. With no party or organizational support, he came close to winning. I admired Silber and felt then that if he won he had a good chance of also winning the presidential nomination in 1992. It is interesting to speculate, five years later, about a President Silber rather than President Clinton.

Oh black seas of Eternity, without height or depth, bay,
brink or shore! How can anyone
look into your depths and neglect
the salvation of his soul?

This non-believer was moved and shaken by these
awful words. They were spoken by an Irish priest
a long time ago and quoted by Hilary Robinson in
her *Somerville and Ross: A Critical Appreciation.*

I read Robinson's book because I had always
been entranced by the work of those two great
Anglo-Irish cousin collaborators, Edith Somerville
and Violet Martin. Their *Experiences of an Irish
R.M.* and *Further Experiences of . . .* (made into a

fine BBC TV serial some years ago) are richly entertaining. They illuminate the whole complex Irish society and I enjoy them more each time I read them.

Herrn
Dr Arnold Genthe
zur herzlichen Erinnerung
René Fülöp-Miller
New York, 1930

I have cited the inscription on the frontispiece of Fülöp Miller's *The Power and Secret of the Jesuits,* a book published by the Viking Press in 1930. The words can be translated in English as "In heartfelt remembrance," and the book itself is apparently a gift from the author to Dr Genthe.

Fülöp-Miller was a gifted Austro-Hungarian intellectual who had studied chemistry at the Sorbonne, philosophy at the University of Vienna and psychiatry with Freud. He interviewed Lenin and then wrote *Lenin and Ghandi; The Mind and Face of Bolshevism; Rasputin: The Holy Devil; The Unknown Tolstoy,* and many other books, both popular and scholarly. He settled in the United States after a visit in 1930, taught Russian civilization and sociology at Dartmouth, and then sociology and anthropology at Hunter College until his retirement in 1962. Fülöp-Miller became an American citizen and died in Hanover, New Hampshire, in 1963.

Arnold Genthe was born in Berlin in 1869, studied classical philology, archaeology and philosophy and received his Ph.D. from the University of Jena. He then spent a year in Paris where he studied French literature and the history of art at the Sorbonne. He came to San Francisco in 1895 as a tutor to the son of a German nobleman. It was then that he became interested in photography and became famous for his portraits. He visited New Mexico and photographed the Hopi, Navajo and Zuñi tribes. In 1911, Genthe moved to New York where many of the famous people of the day sat for his camera. He was one of the first photographers to work with color and his pictures were widely exhibited. He died in New Milford, Connecticut, in 1942, and remains a major figure in the history of photography.

Sadly, these two important cultural figures of the first part of the century are now both virtually forgotten. The material artifacts of any civilization have some chance of survival—after all, with enough digging, one will be faced with the remains of the actual objects that were once in use. There are however, not many traces of cultural artifacts, and now, with the production of so many trillions of words, who can expect even the best to survive? Perhaps only those who have won out in the continual fight for public notice can be remembered.

So it has been at least for Fülöp-Miller and Arnold Genthe, two superb once-prominent European craftsmen, both of whom spent the major part of their lives living and working in the United States. Unfortunately, the quality of their work plays no role in insuring its permanency. Public memory is short and we are left the poorer because of it. To the extent they are remembered today, each is considered neither European nor American. The two cultures did indeed meet, but never merged.

The formal tone of the inscription reminds me of the wistful tale of two other Europeans, Albert Einstein and Thomas Mann. They met at a house party in Princeton, where they discovered that all the guests were expected to call one another by their first names. The two men, at the first opportunity for a private word with each other, were supposed to have agreed that when they were alone each would address the other as "Doctor"! The story is probably apocryphal, but haunting in its evocation of two different cultures.

I remember buying the Fülöp-Miller book in a second-hand bookshop many years ago and I know why I bought it. Miller had been a revered friend of Dick Winston. I met Dick in the Federal prison at Danbury in 1944 where he was serving time as a conscientious objector. We immediately became friends. We played hundreds of chess games together and corresponded until his death in 1980. Dick, together with his novelist wife Clara, became a highly respected translator from the German and the author of a number of fine biographies. I had great respect for Dick and did want to read any book by a writer he admired. But I must confess that I was put off after reading a few pages of Fülöp-Miller's book on the Jesuits and to this day, still haven't finished it.

I guess the main asset an old man has are his memories, and all these were evoked when for some reason I pulled the book from a bookself and once again saw the inscription!

Bibliography

Allen, P.S. *The Age of Erasmus*. New York: Oxford, 1914.

Beer, Thomas. *The Mauve Decade*. New York: Knopf, 1926.

Bettman, Otto L, ed. *Delights of Reading: Quotes, Notes & Anecdotes*. Boston: Godine, 1987.

Bible. *Authorized* or *King James Version*. London: The Nonesuch Press, 1963.

Bible. *New Revised Standard Version*. New York: Oxford, 1989.

Biddle, Francis. *In Brief Authority*. New York: Doubleday, 1962.

Blythe, Ronald. *Akenfield: Portrait of an English Village*. New York: Pantheon, 1969.

Boswell, James. *Boswell's Life of Johnson*. Edited by George Birbeck Hill, 6 vols. London: Oxford, 1887.

Bunyan, John. *Pilgrim's Progress*. New York: Dutton, 1954.

Butler, Samuel. *Erewhon*. Shrewsbury Edition. London: Jonathan Cape, 1872.

———. *The Way of All Flesh*. New York: Heritage Press, 1936.

Chesterfield, Lord. *Letters to His Son*. New York: Tudor, n.d.

Clive, John. *Macauley: The Shaping of the Historian*. Cambridge, Mass.: Belknap Press, 1987.

Cochrane, J.A. *Dr Johnson's Printer: The Life of William Strahan*. London: Routledge & Kegan Paul, 1964.

De Bury, Bishop Richard. *Philobiblon*. London: The De La More Press, 1903.

Dickinson, Lovat. *The House of Words*. New York: Atheneum, 1963.

Dryden, John. *Poetical Works*. Boston: Houghton Mifflin, 1909.

Flexner, James Thomas. *Washington: The Indispensable Man*. Boston: Little, Brown, 1974.

Fraenkel, Heinrich (Aissac). *Adventure In Chess*. London: Turnstile Press, 1951.

Franklin, Benjamin. *Autobiography*. London: Everyman, 1908.

Fülöp-Miller, René. *The Power and Secret of the Jesuits*. New York: Viking, 1930.

Gelderman, Carol. *Louis Auchincloss*. New York: Crown, 1993

Glyn, Jenifer. *Prince of Publishers: A Biography of the Great Victorian Publisher George Smith*. London: Allison & Busby, 1986.

Gray, Arthur. *A Chapter In the Early Life of Shakespeare: Polesworth in Arden.* New York: Cambridge, 1926.

Hacker, Louis M. "The Farmer is Doomed." John Day pamphlets #28, 1933.

Holroyd, Michael. *Bernard Shaw,* Vol. 1: *The Search for Love.* London: Chatto & Windus, 1988.

Horgan, Paul. *A Certain Climate: Essays in History, Arts, and Letters.* Middletown, Conn.: Wesleyan, 1988.

Howatson, M.C., ed. *Oxford Companion to Classical Literature.* New York: Oxford, 1989.

Howe, Mark DeWolfe, ed. *Holmes-Laski Letters.* Cambridge, Mass: Harvard University, 1953.

Huizinga, J. *Erasmus of Rotterdam.* London: Phaidon, 1952.

James, Henry, and Edith Wharton. *Henry James and Edith Wharton: Letters: 1900–1915.* Lyall H. Powers, ed. Scribners, 1990.

Johnson, Paul. *Modern Times*. New York: Harper & Row, 1982.

Junius. *The Junius Letters*, 2 vols. London: T. Bensley for Vernor & Hood, Birchin-Lane, 1794.

King, W. Nephew. *The Story of the Spanish-American War and the Revolt in the Philippines*. New York: Peter Fenelon Collier, 1900.

Lane, Margaret. *Purely for Pleasure*. New York: Knopf, 1967.

Leopardi, Giacomo. *Pensieri*. Baton Rouge, La.: Louisiana State, 1981.

Lewis, D.B. Wyndham. *The Hooded Hawk or the Case of Mr Boswell*. London: Eyre & Spottiswoode, 1946.

Loos, Anita. *Kiss Hollywood Good-Bye*. New York: Viking, 1974.

Lowry, Martin. *The World of Aldus Manutius: Business and Scholarship in Renaissance Venice*. Ithaca, N.Y.: Cornell, 1979.

Martin, George. *The Damrosch Dynasty: America's First Family of Music.* Boston: Houghton Mifflin, 1983.

Mencken, H.L. *H.L. Mencken on Music.* Selected by Louis Cheslock. New York: Knopf, 1961.

Muggeridge, Malcolm. *Chronicles of Wasted Time.* Washington, D.C.: Regnery Gateway, 1972.

Nabokov, Vladimir. *Poems and Problems.* New York: McGraw-Hill, 1970.

Plumb, J.H. "G.M. Trevelyan." Pamphlet published for The British Council and the National Book League. London: Longmans, Green, 1951.

Previn, Andre. *No Minor Chords.* New York: Doubleday, 1991

Raw, Charles, Bruce Page, and Godfrey Hodgson. *Do You Sincerely Want to Be Rich?* New York: Viking, 1971.

Robinson, Hilary. *Somerville and Ross: A Critical Appreciation.* New York: St. Martins, 1980.

Russell, John. *Reading Russell.* New York: Abrams, 1989.

Samuels, Ernest, ed. *Selected Letters of Henry Adams.* Cambridge, Mass.: Harvard University Press.

Schoenbaum, S. *Shakespeare's Lives.* New York: Oxford, 1991.

Shakespeare, William. *The Works.* New York: Shakespeare Head Press, Oxford, 1938.

Silber, John. *Straight Shooting.* New York: Harper and Row, 1989.

Sinclair, Upton. *The Brass Check.* Pasadena, Calif.: Published by the author, 1920.

Slonimsky, Nicolas. *Lectionary of Music.* New York: McGraw Hill, 1989.

Smalley, George W. *London Letters and Some Others.* 2 vols. New York: Harper & Bros., 1891.

Smith, George. *Recollections of a Long and Busy Life.* Unpublished manuscript.

Somerville, E.E., and Martin Ross. *Further Experiences of an Irish R.M.* London: R.S. Surtees Society, 1964.